Academician prof. dr.

MILAN KRAJNC

psychotherapist

HAPPY WE

SUCCESSFUL WE

King & Justus BOOKS

Happy We Successful We

Published by King & Justus Books, LLC
3030 NW Expressway Suite 200 #568
Oklahoma City, OK 73112
www.KingandJustusBooks.com

First Edition
ISBN: 978-1-7349386-9-2

All my books are for her,

The one I was looking for all over the world.

To her, whom I sought in innumerable persons.

To her, which made me climb all the walls and unlock all the doors.

But I didn't find her until I found myself!

And then all of a sudden she showed up, just the way I was looking for her.

All significant things are short
and simple.

Like this book.

It captures the essence of
personal transformation.
The path to success and
happiness is not universal but,
it is related to self-discovery
and decision-making.

The book tells the story of
exactly that path, on which
everyone can make their own
plan from success to happiness.

Table of Contents

FOREWORD

I challenge you to open and read this book with courage.

The moment I read "I ended up a prisoner of my own making" and "When I decided that I would no longer live in pain," I knew that this was someone I could relate to and listen to. The only other person I've said this about is Viktor Frankl because he survived the concentration camps.

From the very start, you are invited into a new world of self-awareness. Sir Dr. Milan Krajnc, a scientist, researcher, writer, psychotherapist, and entrepreneur, reveals, "Only a few know exactly what they feel, what they want, who they are. It all stems from knowing yourself." Pay close attention to his use of the word "exactly." He continues, "The more we know ourselves, the easier it will be for us to manage our time and life."

The way he shares his story and his stories within his story caught me by surprise, partially because our stories are so similar. He shut himself off to finally discover what he truly wanted. His rare vulnerability caused me to trust him, to be drawn to him, to want to be his friend. When he says, "I was blissfully happy," I had tears in my eyes as this was another thing Sir Dr. Milan Krajnc and I have in common.

As the creator of the world's first and only total abundance wellbeing solution, I was excited to see that Sir Dr. Milan Krajnc had also discovered the divine pattern for true success, happiness, peace, and abundance: love, live, give, and enjoy.

The questions contained in the pages ahead will stir every dimension of you. For example, "Who is successful?" and "Why did I never have enough?" and "How ready are you to hear the truth about yourself?" and "Why are the two out of 30 still successful?"

You will experience new insights such as "everything that we do should be to our joy," and "we should never stop in any area in life, but instead live dynamically, as if we were a brook," and not a "swamp." Also, "the problem was not in the choice of occupation, but in the organization I worked for."

Throughout this epic experience, you will more clearly see that love, joy, and peace are intricately interwoven.

Your wisdom improves along this mesmerizingly beautiful journey when he says things like "we need to start within ourselves and only then adapt all external things so that they are in support of our inner vision and feelings. And it is there, right there, where true happiness awaits us." Elsewhere he says to "always set yourself higher goals that will help you to develop continuously and grow." He also says, "No matter how crazy the dreams are, let them begin to live to their fullest."

Be prepared for inspired breakthroughs to happen slowly, then suddenly, when you encounter things like "First, you need to fall in love with yourself, then with life." Also, "The most important thing, however, is to have a true sense of success." Being truly happy is to enjoy your life.

Finally, expect to be empowered as he encourages you to allow your potential to develop freely and shows you how to become the master of your own destiny.

From start to finish, this book will take you "from the surface to the depths" and reveal "the right path to happiness" so you can at last "start living dynamically and fully."

Prioritize taking a 2-day retreat to learn how to love, live, give, and enjoy. Furthermore, Sir Dr. Milan Krajnc writes, "Setting yourself in your own true life of happiness and satisfaction is a long-lasting process." But this is far better than waking up one day in your fake life "successful in the eyes of others," but unhappy at the same time.

By the time you're finished reading and reflecting, the idea that "happiness is the key to life" simply won't mean what it did before. I will mean far more.

Not everyone will listen, but those who do will say, "Wow."

Rick Justus

Founder & Chairman, King & Justus,
Preeminent Creator of Abundant Leaders and Economies

WE, SUCCESSFUL?

In the eyes of most people, I am *successful*. Personally, I do not have that feeling. I would instead say that I am constantly in some sort of turbulence. I notice that also in other people who are—like me—considered *successful*.

For that reason, I decided to investigate this phenomenon. Who is *successful?* I too consider some to be successful and others not so much; so I decided to take an in-depth look into their subconscious, into their life.

- Why are they successful?
- Do they feel unsuccessful, too?
- What is their goal anyway?
- Why are they in such a hurry if they are already successful?
- Why do they set such high goals?
- Who are the *successful*?

I took myself as the first example because it is the fastest way to gather most information.

Otherwise, I would write about others from my perspective; however, this would not be a credible depiction. It is hard to talk about yourself because you cannot remain objective. Nevertheless, talking about others is also not realistic since we are not in their shoes. What is realistic, anyway? All I can consider realistic is what I feel at a given moment, since feelings set us apart from the inanimate world. Our senses reflect our state. That is why it is essential to keep the sensors clean. On the following pages, we inspect:

- what affects our well-being,
- how we can ourselves influence our well-being,
- how it is even possible to clean the sensors so that we are able to *come clean* at all times.

The most important thing, however, is to have a true sense of success.

How ready are you
to hear the truth
about yourself?
Because afterwards
there is no going
back!

HOW MUCH DO I NEED TO EARN TO BE HAPPY?

Lately, I have been touring abroad and giving lectures outside Slovenia. After one lecture on happiness, an attendee said to me, "You know, those people you talked about **indeed feel happy, but they're not successful.**" He listed a few criteria he felt were necessary for success, from ranking high on the social ladder, owning a company with hundreds of employees, and having at least a few million dollars in the bank.

"And how do these *successful* people feel at the end of the day?", I asked him, as it was clear from his views that he had specific individuals in mind.

"Well," he continued in a less convincing voice, "maybe they really are a bit tired, they've had enough of everything, since all that isn't that simple...".

"And why do you think they do all that?", I asked further.

"So that they could be at peace one day!"

And so, we ended the conversation, because he answered his question of what it means to be *happy*.

I have pondered the question of what it means to be happy. I also often wondered what the purpose of all this work.

I wondered why I had not continued working at school where I would finish my day at noon, receive a steady salary and be the biggest local hotshot in town. Why did I want more? Already at the age of 24, I quit my job and entered entrepreneurial waters. The company snowballed. At one point, we had more than 3,000 employees on the team.

Why did I have to substitute my peaceful life as a teacher and become someone who was under heavy stress every day and was on the receiving end of at least ## swear words a day? Why did I have to go into public life after that? Why did I have to enter the battle for the highest official positions after that? Why did I never have enough? At one point, I wondered in astonishment "When will I ever have enough?"

My workdays lasted 24 hours and were interrupted by waking up with hemorrhages. I knew it was not right for me, but I went a little further every day, comforting myself saying, "Just one more thing and I'm done, and then just one more thing ..." But this *"just one more thing"* never ended. It was never enough. Even in the moments when I wanted to stop, I could not. How could I? I was responsible for all employees at a large company. Every month, funds had to be provided for the company and for the employees. I felt like I was working only for others. Although on the outside I seemed like a millionaire with thousands of employees, the truth was different. Often everyone around me had at least that steady salary, while I could barely afford petrol.

How did I get here? When I looked back at, it became clear that I was not happy as a teacher. However, the problem was not in the choice of occupation, but in the organization. Nevertheless, I did not complain, but instead took responsibility and destiny in my own hands. And consequently, I left. I struck out on my own.

It was a journey. As a result, I opened a path to all my demons which simply spread out all over the world and all over my body. Each of them made its home, its environment and I ended up a prisoner of my own making.

I used to be a prisoner in another system, and now I was a prisoner of others in myself (demons are psychological patterns that my environment instilled in me in early childhood). Only when I was so exhausted by the demons that I could no longer breathe, I began to ask myself *Who am I really; what do I really want* ... and not what others advise me to do or expect from me.

What did I want as a child? A child who is not yet burdened by the pressures of the surroundings. In my early childhood, I told myself that I would make a living from writing and lecturing. I took that path. But even though I wrote and lectured, there was not enough.

In all this refection on my life, I one day received my personal medical report with alarming red flags. The report scared me more than bank statements in the red ever did. All I had left was to go bankrupt both professionally and privately, which meant those were the last moments of my life in this world.

This is when I, one day, withdrew from public and social life. I was nowhere to be found. I cut all contacts with everyone. I shut myself off to finally find the answer to the question of what I truly want:

Do I want to live? YES.

Do I want to live a quality life? YES.

Do I want to live my childhood dreams? YES.

I started systematically writing and updating my old texts. Book after book began to emerge. Writing became my cleansing, my therapy. And only now am I clean enough to be able to start teaching and lecturing; my whole journey was in its core nothing but the cleansing of myself. I had to walk the path to get to where I am now.

Because now when I am about to start teaching, the information must be clean. Otherwise, I will pass on *tainted* information to the audience. I want to clean the environment to create a healthy environment. And only now that I am healthy, it is possible for me to do so. Only now I can teach about the meaning of life and happiness!

However, my contemplation does not end there. I would like to provide an answer to the question referred to in the title of the chapter, "How much do I need to earn to be happy? Where is that limit?"

Yesterday I came across the following news:

"First photos of two suicide bombers behind Easter Sunday bombings in Sri Lanka published."

The footage of the attack shows that the attackers entered the hotel unnoticed while numerous guests were at breakfast; just a moment later, the two hotel restaurants turned into a sight of horror.

Inshaf and Ilham Ibrahim quietly entered the Shangri-La and Cinnamon Grand hotels and detonated explosives attached to their vests, killing hotel guests who came for Easter breakfast.

The wealthy brothers killed more than 40 foreigners who were on vacation, among them also were three children.

Just hours later, police entered the lavish home of Ilham's pregnant wife Fatima, who then set of another bomb and blew up herself, her three children up, and three police officers.

The Ibrahim brothers were the sons of a spice merchant and millionaire Jonus Ibrahim and were educated at private schools in Colombo.

Neighbours considered the family modern and there were no indications pointing to their affiliation with extremists.

Inshaf lived with his wife and children in a house worth £1.5 million in the elite part of Colombo.

On the day he decided to kill innocent people, Inshaf told his wife that he was going on a business trip and that she should be brave.

Alaudin, Inshaf's father-in-law and the owner of the house where the attacker lived with his family, said in shock after the tragedy, "He had everything—a good job, a wonderful wife and four beautiful children. Why would he do something like that?"

Alaudin added that his son-in-law never mentioned the Islamic State and that he never suspected that Inshaf could develop any sympathy for extremists.

The above vividly illustrates the state of our society. At some point, people lose the meaning of life. We simply become fed-up with everything, - having already achieved everything -and do not know where to go next. The two young men from the article above found new meaning in faith, in some higher goal. Nevertheless, they were dealing with someone higher, instead of dealing with themselves.

This is why the only way to save society and to save ourselves is to look deep inside and ask ourselves, "Who am I? What do I feel? Where am I going?"

This will give us the answer to the question, "How much do I need to earn to be happy?" **As much as we will need for our journey, the journey that will be travelled free of stress and worries.**

Any search for the meaning of life outside oneself – somewhere else, proving oneself to others, competing with them –is an imaginary world. The only true world and the only right path – the one within you.

Start dealing with your feelings, not other people – each moment, each hour, each day at a time. You will have so much to do with yourself that you will not be interested in people around you anymore. You will have the feeling of living in the moment, in eternity. You will live!

Be like nature –
everything is perfect
as long as it lives ...

DOES SUCCESS EQUAL HAPPINESS?

Through my life stories and professional knowledge, I will try to demonstrate what it really means to be successful, how to become successful, and when is the right time.

As a scientist, researcher, writer, psychotherapist, and an entrepreneur, I have been dealing with the successes of other entrepreneurs for 20 years. Above all, I am interested in why they are successful, what all influences their decisions, and how they think. In fact, I have always been interested in the mindset of winners. I largely compared them to athletes. And was that success is a burden to someone and a delight to others. I did not understand that at first. It became clear to me only after I had conducted a series of interviews with the most successful entrepreneurs who were awarded the highest prizes in their area of expertise, only then to slowly disappear from the entrepreneurial world. I have analyzed more than 20 such winners.

What interested me most was why these winners were no longer engaged in entrepreneurship, considering they had already achieved the highest success in their industry.

They could not provide me with a straightforward answer. Interestingly, their answers were very similar. They simply no longer felt satisfaction in entrepreneurship, or they somehow got lost and did not know how to move forward.

After a detailed discussion and comparative analyses, I concluded that all of them had the same *pain point*. In their early childhood, they grew up without a father or with a strict father and were rarely, or some even, never praised — they were simply never good enough.

They spent their lives continuously longing for approval. In fact, it was the longing that was exhausting to them and success soon a burden to them as well. Despite that, they could not *help themselves*, since something was forcing them to keep pushing forward until they became the richest, the most recognizable, present in the media every day, the best in every field. Everyone envied their success, but in reality, it was a burden to them. Regardless of all the success, wealth, and recognition, deep inside themselves, they felt unhappy and many times lonely.

When they were shortlisted for the most prestigious award, that *invisible force* in them almost went wild. The moment they heard their name, saw their picture on the screen, an explosion happened in them that took them onto the stage. They received the award — proud and happy. They listened to praises on their behalf. However, the very next moment, the invisible force in them slowly began to disappear. Suddenly, they felt lost on that stage, like imposters, they did not really know what they were doing there at all and would have rather just ran away.

The next morning, the media were flooded with their name more than ever before. And yet, they felt utterly lost, as if they were no longer the same person, as if they had fallen from another planet, as if as if they were in some game, in some other show ... they wondered *where* they were and *who* they were.

Now that their businesses were facing even greater outbursts of success, they simply could no longer think of a reason why they should have the business at all and continue doing what they do. They slowly began to retreat; their businesses slowly began to shut down, friends and families started abandoning them and they themselves withdrew into complete isolation.

As I listened to them, I assumed the reward was in fact equal to the praise of the father they had so longed for all their lives and that invisible force was, in reality, the pain that pushed them towards finally having to experience their moment. And once that moment happened, the pain they experienced would disappear.

These conversations confirmed that most of the things they did were not for themselves, but their *father*. These people were between 40 and 50 years old, which means they were carrying that burden for more than 30 years, only to wake up one day in their fake lives.

Everything they bought, everything they did, everything they aspired to — all that was just to please others. Of course, they were tired of success. Although they were *successful* in the eyes of others, they were at the same time *unhappy*. It was all in the subconscious with the desire for validation and satisfaction of their father's voice — ***you are not good enough***! In fact, they were looking for their father in people around them and all those who bore any resemblance with or reminded them in any way of him in their behaviour. This was all done with a deep subconscious desire to feel what they did not receive in their childhood. And that exact pain brought them to the very top of the world of the successful. Nevertheless, the reward that fed that pain eventually threw them back to the bottom right to the point from which they started or from which they were supposed to start on their own.

Two of these award winners I was examining are still prospering and expanding their businesses, thus my attention focused on them as well. I was curious about what the key difference between the two of them and the others. Why are the two still *successful*?

As they told their life story, I did not observe that they ever had any limitations in their childhood. That does not mean that they had everything available and that they could do whatever came to their minds, but rather that their parents encouraged and accepted them. I got the impression that they grew up in a happy and healthy environment and that they precisely developed the way they felt. Their parents taught them to live the way they feel.

It was evident that they were happy. They enjoyed their job, and they enjoyed their life. They did not pay attention to their media image. They thought it was more important to have their products and satisfied customers in the foreground, but above all their employees. They were aware of the following: the more satisfied their employees are, the more time they will have for themselves and will be concerned only with what makes them truly happy.

When I would occasionally meet some of the employees of the entrepreneurs who are no longer *on the scene*, I would mostly hear negative things, such as manipulation, intimidation, pressure, and exploitation. However, from the outside, the company had an outstanding image, radiated brilliance and was a role model.

On the other hand, when talking to the employees working in the companies of the two satisfied entrepreneurs, I realised that everything was very relaxed. What mattered was that the work was done well and on time, while it was irrelevant when the employees came to work. They were free from all pressures, despite the fact that there was nevertheless some order respected.

The situation quickly brought to my mind an association to nature. I am a physicist and a technician, only later did I get involved in economics and business, which meant that whenever something was unclear to me, I would look for an analogy in natural or technical phenomena. In nature too there are no pressures, and yet everything happens exactly when it should and exactly as it should. It seemed to me that these two happy entrepreneurs did everything in a certain natural rhythm, while with the others were working in opposition to the ease of nature, which is why ultimately everything under them fell apart.

Comparing the natural way of working and working under pressure, it began to dawn on me what it means when you associate *success* with pressure, and what it means on the other hand when *success* is considered a logical consequence of your work. At this point I began to explore what was actually going on in the human subconscious. In other words, after studying physics, I continued my studies in psychology and psychotherapy.

Our upbringing (or surrounding environment) has a massive impact on us in early childhood, all the way up to the sixth year of growing up. A child is not born with instructions for life, but is instead born with specific potentials and instincts, which intuitively develops by imitating surroundings. That is why it is crucial for the child how that environment lives. If the latter lives in accordance with its feelings, the child will also imitate that and live what is felt inside, in other words, the child will allow their potential to develop freely. We call that *live and work with the heart*. However, if the child grows up in an environment filled with limitations and countless bans, they will suppress their potential and live by the instructions, expectations and demands of others.

That is why it is not crucial in how *rich* the family we are born into but rather and above all in how *free* the family is in which we are born.

John Lennon said, "When I was five years old, my mother always told me that happiness was the key to life. When I went to school, they asked me what I wanted to be when I grew up. I wrote down 'happy.' They told me I didn't understand the assignment, and I told them they didn't understand life."

This means that it is not necessary to be born as an entrepreneur, instead, our dreams that we must not restrain from take us to entrepreneurship. No matter how crazy the dreams are, let them begin to live to their fullest.

This is how on my 20-year entrepreneurial journey as a researcher and psychotherapist I have seen just how many people live in wretchedness and pain, despite having the solution all the time right there in front of them. But still they could not see it because all the wrong guidance they had received in their childhood was so strong that it almost ruined their lives.

Fran Milčinski Ježek wrote, *"It hurts when we are run over by a car, but when we get run over by time, the pain cannot be measured."*

When we are born, everything we receive is a gift, everything but time; and it only depends on us how we use the time. We do not have time to spare. That is why it is important how we live, who we keep company with, and what and who we dedicate our time. In fact, the greatest gift you can give to someone is the time that you dedicate to them – thus dedicating them a part of your life.

For this reason, it is pointless to keep learning from your own mistakes, as I myself repeatedly did. That is why in the book, *Wisdom for Those Who Want to Live*, I wrote:

"Follow my advice, so you don't make the same mistakes I made."

The purpose of the manual is not to offer a step-by-step guide to success (or happiness), but rather a pre-preparation and a different view of a way of thinking.

Think carefully before making any decision. Always make long-term decisions. First, look at how that decision will affect you and only then your surroundings. The order is important: YOU first, then others. However, even though *the others* are in the second place, you must never forget about them.

That is why it is essential to keep your thoughts clear when making decisions. You can achieve clearness with high morals and ethics, for which this whole book is based.

When we say that we live someone else's life, it means that we live according to the patterns of those who represent our authority, such as parents, educators or individuals who have a certain impact on us. However, we also absorb their habits, and not just the good things that we like, but rather the complete package. And since the complete package means a foreign body in us, we will constantly have problems with it in our future life. For the foreign body to feel good, it will require validation or attention from where it came from, bringing us into a frequent conflict with ourselves and our surroundings. That means living someone else's life — these are the foreign bodies, psychological litter, complexes, demons — no matter what the name it is given, it is something that does not belong in us.

All of you who feel
sorry for yourself
because you got lost,
deep down inside
you know very well
your path.
Could you get lost
if you didn't know
where you were
going?

I USED TO BE A CHILD ... AS DID YOU.

Childhood has an enormous impact on our lives. In fact, early childhood upbringing determines the key direction we are going to take on life's path. Therefore, in the following steps, we will focus on how life is usually steered into a particular direction and how we can later influence our life by removing all the litter that others have piled into our minds and bodies.

Having a *tough* childhood, since alcohol provoked aggression in my father which he would then release in the family circle, never embark on a similar path. Nevertheless, all these events influenced me to shut myself off from the world at that moment. That is how I created a safe refuge for my dreams; and I was dreaming big.

Although I would often leave a strange impression when explaining my desires and dreams, I never allowed myself to have them taken away from me or have them compromised by anyone. My environment in particular was trying to persuade me that the world is not what I dream.

And if I look back on those years today, I can confirm that my childhood had an enormous impact on me. Then, at some point, when I decided that I would no longer live in pain, I found strength from that pain. My pain became a tool. I began to discover why pain occurs, how to deal with it, and how to overcome it. One of the outcomes of this process is this book.

What would
a child that
you once
used to be
say about
the person
you grew
up to be?

On the following pages, I provide a practical example that illustrates how psychological patterns are transmitted and how certain issues that have been in us since our early youth can be overcome.

CHILDREN – REFLECTION OF THEIR PARENTS

"How difficult the director is today! She's been nagging me the whole time to tidy up my desk. But all I have there are the things that are necessary for my daily work. Okay, maybe it really seems like a lot, but I really need almost everything. And with the system that I have, I always know where things are. I really don't understand why she keeps nagging me! Her desk is so clean as if she is not working at all. That's why she doesn't have the slightest clue about what creative chaos is." That is what one of the project managers at the marketing agency was telling me about yesterday. Today we met again for a talk, but this time we left the office building to get some fresh air. This made our conversation more relaxed.

He carefully hinted at his request to not report him to the director because of what he said against her.

Without hesitation, I assured him that he could have full confidence in me. We sat down on a park bench next to a brook and sipped our coffees. We watched the water of the brook. He said how he liked this freshness of the water, especially because the brook flowed just fast enough to create around it a relaxed and refreshing atmosphere. Not far from us, we could hear children's voices. He turned around and added that he had two such rascals at home.

I asked him how they got along. "Until recently, it was a disaster, but now we get along great. I hope that it also stays that way," he replied. I asked him what exactly he meant by that. Besides a few remarks about the typical disobedience of children, he mentioned that "Those little troublemakers used to have a room so messy that it looked like a bomb went off inside. I have absolutely no clue how they managed to find anything in there. They even claimed to have such a system by which they always knew where things were ... When my wife and I tidied their room, they went berserk. They accused us of getting two unexcused absences at school because of us. Since they didn't have everything for school with them, the teachers sent them home. And they of course didn't have the things because they couldn't find them at home. They accused us of destroying their lives, that we didn't understand them, and that we should let them organise their things on their own. I really don't know who they got that from, since my wife and I have everything very neat and tidy. We really keep things in order at home."

I looked him straight in the eyes and asked, "Does their room perhaps remind you of your desk at work?"

"No," he replied quickly, but then he held his breath. "Well, maybe really a little ... But they have never been in my office, they have never seen it, how could they then possibly be doing the same thing?!"

Children are not born with instructions for life, but instead learn by observing others. This is what we call raising by setting an example. The human psyche is made so that it is formed adapted to the one it is raising. That person represents the child's authority. Regardless of how the person treats themselves, the child will imitate their behaviour. This imitation takes place in the first six years of our lives. In that period, the human character is formed or the life scenario by which we spend the rest of our life is written.

After we processed all these transferred patterns, he added at the end, "Just yesterday, I was sitting with my wife on the terrace drinking coffee when the boys approached us and thanked us for cleaning up their room. We were very surprised because only a few days before we thought that in all their rage, they would kick us out of the house. And then a complete twist. Where is this *thank you* coming from, we asked the children. They replied that it is now much easier for them to find their things faster. But most surprisingly, what they noticed about themselves was that they had become much calmer and more creative, that is creative in a positive sense, since even the teacher praised them, which had never happened before."

Before he continued, as a comparison, I explained to him how the basic memory works of the computers we use every day. Computer memory is like a large space in which we daily enter or open large amounts of data. As the amounts keep increasing, we need more and more time to find a certain piece of information. This is because we move and misplace the information. In short, the pile of information we are always searching through keeps growing. Over time, overloaded with data, our computers start running slower. The instructions on the use of the computer require us to run at least once a week the application that cleans this data-overloaded space. And this is how the computer works faster.

He looked at me. "Are you saying I should tidy up my desk?" He understood quickly. However, he resisted the change by asking,

"Don't you understand that I find things faster now because I know the system?"

"How long have you had all that stuff on your desk?" I asked him.

"Ever since I've been at the company."

"And how long has that been?"

"Five years."

I looked at him a little perplexed and asked if he did not think that five-year-old documents were already outdated.

"Some maybe, but our projects are linked to each other and so it is good to have them at hand."

Our conversation stopped. After a while, when we had already finished our coffees in that relaxed environment surrounded by the bubbling sounds of the nearby brook, breathing in the freshness of nature, I asked him, "Can we review the contents of the documents on your desk together?"

"Of course, I'll be happy to," he replied and added, "We can do it right now."

We took one last sip of coffee and headed back to his office. After three hours of reviewing the documents, we made three piles. The first pile had documents to be written off, the second one contained archives and folders, while the third pile had documents arranged by priority, with deadlines, by which respective document needed to be finished, written on each of them. He suddenly realised that even in 14 days the documents would no longer be on his desk. It was already 3:30 p.m., the end of workday, so I invited him for another coffee. We sat down by the brook again.

It took him a few deep breaths and moments of silence to think before he mustered the courage for a sincere confession. "Before I felt refreshed here, but now I feel calm and light. What have you done to me?"

"What do you think I did? The same thing you did to your sons. I cleaned up! Remember, when I told you how computer memory works? If you want it to work smoothly, you have to tidy it up every week. If you had not done that for five years, it would have become very chaotic and slow. And this is exactly the state your desk, but also your subconscious, was in. Your subconscious mind acts similar to a computer memory. You have to tidy it up too. By clearing your desk, you also cleared your subconscious. Now you no longer have to keep all the data in mind and keep track of which pile hides the exact piece of information you need. This means you have also cleared some space in your mind. There is not so much load anymore and your head is suddenly breathing. That is why you feel calm and lighter."

He understood what we achieved by tidying up.

"How can such ease and peace be achieved permanently? What can I do so that I don't forget these principles and start piling things up on my desk again?" he wondered.

"The answer to that question can be found in nature. If we only look at this brook in front of us." I pointed with my hand towards the stream that was murmuring in front of us. "We see how clear it is and how refreshing the atmosphere it creates is. For that fishpond at the end of the park, which looks more like a swamp, we have already established that it is not of a particularly pleasant smell, not to mention it is impossible to talk about its clarity. **If we want to**

be clear, we must create the conditions in which things constantly flow. There can be no standstills, or a swamp starts to form.

All you have to do now is start working on the projects that land on your desk and finish them within the agreed deadlines."

"You're right," he agreed. However, I could feel already in his voice his hesitation lingering, "But it's not all up to me. The colleague in the next-door office needs to do his job as well. And that is why I had so many projects on my desk since his documents are not sorted, and then I browse through those documents myself."

Since I knew where his colleague was sitting, I asked him: "Wouldn't it be better to keep your office doors open or maybe even share an office?"

"Anything would be possible, however, that cannot be done because of the infrastructure."

"Okay, I understand." I gave up at that moment. The next morning, I talked to the company director on how to improve communication among employees and already in the afternoon of the same day, the workers removed the office wall barrier. That is how they got one big, spacious office and the communication between the two started running smoothly.

A week later, all three of us were sitting having coffee at the already known location in nature. What has changed? Much. They were both extremely pleased with the change. We then discussed what was before this current state. Why such chaos on work desks? We agreed that before we had created the shared space office plan, there was a *communication swamp* between them. And as this space was non-functional, the *swamp* began to form on their desks. They ended up needing too much data for a certain use.

Further on, the *swamp* appeared in their heads as well because they had to think about the same things over and over again. When they looked at the whole company from that perspective, they found out that they had one huge *swamp* in the company. They flinched at the realisation of the solution.

"You have it right in front of you. The solution is in the flow of the brook," I said. **Work process should flow too so that every business move and every business person is *clear*.**

An overload of information leads to information *puddles*. That is why it is necessary to air well the whole company.

In our relaxed conversation, we digressed into philosophical waters a bit. We began to identify the numerous similarities between nature and real life. A pool of water is created in nature due to water stagnation, and then various animals that are not pleasing to the eye begin to be born from it ... It is most unpleasant to look at frogspawns and frogs. That is how also within companies, unpleasant things start to appear from their *communication swamps*. And from their *soul swamps* unpleasant thoughts begin to emerge. If we do not have the right and timely information, fears and doubts begin to arise — *what is happening, surely someone hates us, wants to get rid of us, is setting us up*. All those uncomfortable thoughts only because we do not have all the information. That is how swamps can become dangerous and can even turn into *wetlands*.

Communication swamps in a company cause duplication of work and unevenly distributed responsibilities.

Of course, the question that followed immediately was how to ensure that the flow in the company never stops.

All this concerns primarily the individual. Delays first start in our heads, not on our desks, not in our offices, but in us. This is why we first have to set ourselves *in motion*. We need to start living dynamically and fully. Humans are, by nature, rather in warm than cold environment. If we measure the temperature in the brook and in the swamp, we see that the swamp is much warmer. That is why people prefer to stay in swamps. However, we tend to forget that over time, swamps acquire an unpleasant smell, which we ourselves do not sense until others start avoiding us.

For this reason, we should never stop in any area in life, but instead live dynamically, as if we were a brook. We have to keep swimming all the time, so we do not become cold and that we do not let the current carry us as it wants.

And such is our life — it can be like a swamp or like a brook.

After four hours of talking, we said to ourselves that it was time to slowly move from words to action. In today's society, there is generally too much talk and too little action. That too is one of the main causes for the formation of *swamps*. This is beautifully described in the Italian proverb, "*Tra il dire ed il fare c'è di mezzo il mare*," which translates into, "**Between saying and doing there is half a sea**."

When we came to the office the following morning, we took upon ourselves to make sure that there would never be any *swamps* in this company again. We started implementing in the company the dynamic model of communication. The basis of the model is the *flow of the brook*, i.e., creating a flow of information that assures the director's idea is carried out practically unchanged by the last person in the process. Communication in the company became easier, the talks were clearer and more concise, and employees performed fewer tasks but achieved more. Pressure and stress reduced, disagreements almost disappeared, and tensions eased. We could say that everything ran with less effort, with a fresh impetus, smoother, and clearer – just like that clear water brook with a constant influx of fresh water.

(You can read more on how we achieved this in the book, *The Dynamic Business Leadership Model*.)

And from here on we live happily and successfully for the rest of our lives?

It is not that simple ...

Not even sunlight can
reach the Earth when
there is too much
smog in the air.

FROM THE SURFACE TO THE DEPTHS

The journey we have taken so far is only *opening the eyes* to finally see everything that was covered in litter. We can imagine it as though wiping the dust off a surface that remains the same, but it is somehow more beautiful. It is cleaner. It is fresher. Of course, it is now also easier to spot every cut, every crack, every irregularity, and every deeper stain. And although we feel that everything is different now, it is only a "psychological trick." Only now can we really see what we need to change.

When I met the following week with the same employee from the previous story, he said that it was now far easier to work, that everything seemed clearer, and that he only now recognised that in the past he had lived the life of others, since it was that *litter* that was a kind of food for others. He began to feel that an external weight was off his shoulders, however, another void started to appear.

He began to feel his own emptiness, his own hunger. He did not know how to explain nor understand it, but he had the impression that his life was now more terrible. Anxiety overcame him and he could barely breathe.

He screamed inside himself, "I have lost my life! Who am I? What am I? What is happening? Why this void? Why all these terrible feelings? Everything is lost!" I reassured him by saying that as long as he was breathing, nothing was lost. Only when he stops breathing, then will it really be too late. Thus, we focused on what he actually felt. We talked about what he perceives as pleasure.

We concluded that he did not feel anything at all. All the feelings he had had thus far were the feelings he learned from his surroundings or films. He had a wedding just like from a movie, and yet he was dissatisfied. Due to his position in the company, he had a high enough salary to be able to afford the material luxury, but still he was not satisfied. He had everything that he saw in the movies and in others necessary to be happy. However, now that he had wiped the dust off his life, he realised that many of those things represented a burden to him. All these material things require from him maintenance and constant updates to always remain successful in the eyes of others. Always looking for more, better, newer, more expensive ... Where does it all lead?!

He realised in horror, saying " In fact, it's only now that I'm aware of how I've been living all along. I was pleasing others. By doing so I was losing the feeling of living. In fact, I didn't even live. I was a prisoner and I let others *feed* on my life energy!"

Great. **The first step is acknowledgement.** The dust has been wiped off and thus a view of one's own personality, one's own inside, one's own sincere feelings finally made possible.

"But, what now? I don't know what to do next!"

Your self-respect is
your contribution
to the development
of society.
Only when you get
to know yourself are
you able to honestly
ask someone:
"How are you?"

WHO ARE YOU?

The answer to the question of who we really are and where we are going is clear to us already in very early childhood. Due to all the expectations of our surroundings, we very quickly forget it.

Let us look at the case of the employee from the previous story who I, after he had already tidied up his desk and cleared his swamps, took back to his childhood in the next step. "What did you dream of when you were a little boy? What was it that made you feel good?"

Out of the blue, he replied, "I danced to the music!"

"Did you ever dance after that?" "Yes, the whole primary and secondary school. At university, I took up folklore and I enjoyed it immensely."

"And today?"

"Well, not really … My wife was never a fan of it, as she is more into the Viennese waltz and tango … I'm not saying they aren't nice, I do let myself fall into the rhythm, but in folklore I feel like I'm in touch with my ancestors, there is energy coming from my cells, I actually feel myself as a whole."

"So, you're also a prisoner of your marriage." He paused a bit, pondered, looked at the floor, and in the end quietly admitted, "Yeah, in a way I am."

"Would you really like to get rid of everything that burdens you?" I challenged him.

He remained quiet.

"Try to answer the following questions by next week and maybe then you will also get your answer:

- How do you feel in your new car?
- How do you feel when you think of folklore?
- How do you feel when you sleep with your wife?
- How do you feel when you are on a walk along a brook in nature?"

And we said goodbye.

Exactly a week later, he came to me in a completely different mood. He appeared very satisfied, but at the same time looking as if he was going to die any minute.

Before I said anything to him, he started telling me that being with his wife made him feel the way he felt when being in his car. And then he paused. He became even paler.

"But in nature, I feel the same way as when dancing the folklore." Suddenly, he was revived, his cheeks turning red, and he smiled from ear to ear. "And it was exactly this feeling that was slowly developing throughout the week. When I thought that I would have to leave my wife and my car, I felt sick to my stomach ... Yet, the joy that I had not felt since my childhood kept growing every moment."

He began to laugh. "This is exactly the feeling I would like to have at all times." I let him calm down.

"Great;" I was finally able to say a word. "But now it is also necessary to start maintaining this feeling. Now it is gushing like oil from the depths, but if you don't do anything with it, if you don't direct the feeling properly, it won't have any value. Just like oil won't, if we don't start extracting and processing it properly."

"What am I supposed to do? I can't just sell my car, replace my wife and dance all day!"

"No need to do that. You don't have to change your car for a worse one. You only have to change the way you look at it. It used to be a status symbol to you and a way of showing off before your neighbours, but now consider it a car that is safe and functional.

You also shouldn't just leave your wife either. Start talking to her about your feelings. Maybe she also feels like she is in a new car. Just as you sorted out the communication issue in your company, you must also sort it out with your wife. And only when all the litter that has piled up between the two of you is removed, you will see exactly what to do next. Maybe she too wants the same. Start talking about feelings and emotions. And above all, start living them."

I saw him struggling with hundreds of thoughts and questions in his head.

"But, you know, everything we have needs to be maintained, so a lot needs to be done."

I interrupted him in the middle of his explanation and asked firmly:

- "Do you enjoy this job? NO!
- Do you need all these material things? NO!
- Do you need all such big things? NO!"

So?

Start thinking about what makes you happy. What job and which position would make you feel good? What do you really need to maintain that sense of satisfaction?

Do not expect miracles overnight. The life we have been building for 15, 25, 50 or more years cannot be changed in one night. **Setting yourself in your own true life of happiness and satisfaction is a long-lasting process.** Even if you want it done tomorrow, it is not possible because it is necessary to make a safe transition.

People make a great mistake because as they sense the moment of *liberation*, they want to change everything in a moment. They would rather immediately delete everything, quit their job, leave their partner, replace their house and car, maybe even the country ... and start it all over again. However, that is not the right approach. The feelings of the first liberation are not yet real feelings. Making such hasty decisions causes even more damage.

First of all, it is necessary to think about and leave an open path to all those desires regarding what we want, who we are, and where we want to go. Only when these desires are balanced do we begin to discover ourselves and what we actually want.

It is important to put our personal goal first. Only then do we look around ourselves. And only then can we realistically look at business projects, the space in which we live, how we live, the people we socialize with and with whom we share our bed. Do all of these support our personal goal? If the answer is YES, then nothing needs to be changed, only harmonised.

After many conversations and even more self-searching, he quickly realised that the more he knows himself, the easier it will become for him to choose the way he works, the people he surrounds himself with, the way he lives, and what he eats. Only in this way will he be able to maintain the feeling of satisfaction.

This is the right path to happiness - the inside out. It never works in the opposite direction. But that is exactly what most do — they buy material things and change partners, locations, jobs, before they stop and look at themselves. It does not work that way. We need to start within ourselves and only then adapt all external things so that they are in support of our inner vision and feelings. And it is there, right there, where the true happiness awaits us.

First, you need to fall
in love with yourself,
then with life...and
then nothing but
love remains around
you.

THE EFFECT OF SURROUNDINGS

As we have seen, in personal and business transformations, we reach a stage when our surrounding environment begins to notice our changes. Some like it, others do not. In what way and how much should we pay attention to those we love most?

An entrepreneur in his mature years was telling me about his success story, which, however, was not always worthy of being called *successful*.

"As a child, I was building model airplanes all the time. I graduated from woodworking secondary school, passed the pilot's exam and finished my mechanical studies. Yes, I was actually a pilot. Yet, I continued to build model airplanes. I built them myself, all sorts of them. My favourite was the zeppelin, which is still in use today. During my first flights with the national airline, I met my future wife, who was the chief flight attendant on those flights. We liked each other already at first sight, but she probably noticed me more because of my uniform and position. I didn't think of it at the time, but she did often point out how proud she was of me when she would see me stepping off the plane in my uniform.

We had two children together and our family was perfect. Well, at least from the outside it was. We really lacked nothing, as we were financially stable, with a high social status, with my wife bright, young, and beautiful. Despite all that, I no longer felt as happy as I did in the beginning, before I started working and got married. Over time, I no longer liked the uniform and the position I had in society. I don't know why. In fact, it was all too much for me. More and more, I found myself closed off in my workshop, where I would enjoy immensely making my airplane models. One day, I summed up the potential income I could get from the sale of the models and realised that I could also make a living from it, and most importantly, I really loved doing this job! So, I decided that I would no longer be a pilot, but instead make airplane models. How excited I was! That's it, that's where I'll find my happiness again!

Well, so it was, until I approached my wife ... I told her what I had decided, and she went crazy. I had never before seen such a facial expression on her. She was like a completely different person! It was as though somebody took off her beautiful mask behind which hid a completely different and not at all a benevolent being. It was really terrifying being on the receiving end of all her rage. Eventually, she said 'Do what you want, just earn enough so we can keep living the way we have lived so far!'

Deeply hurt, I then withdrew myself to my workshop, where I remained for days on end—not only because I wanted to run away from my wife, but also because I actually needed to work much harder to maintain the same financial standard.

Of course, I eventually asked myself what that standard was in reality, was it worth it, where was all the money I had earned, and was money really more important to my wife than I was?

But it was my wife who in the end decided for me. There came the day when she told me that she had found another man and that she could no longer live with me like that. She replaced me with another uniform – a doctor's uniform.

I was left alone, without money, energy or motivation for work and life. I really thought it had all come to an end. However, I was found by a woman who was looking for me because she heard I was crafting amazing things, and she wanted to meet me. At first, we just talked, soon we started a business partnership, and somewhere along the way we fell in love and got married.

In a few months, my life changed completely. I continued to make model airplanes, but only as many as I felt were enough to my personal satisfaction, while my wife was selling them through her company at a very high price in Russia and Australia. I was blissfully happy. Next to me was a person who accepted me for who I was, and I could do exactly what I wanted to. I couldn't imagine that all that was possible. I used to work fifteen hours a day and there still wouldn't be enough of everything, I was extremely miserable. Now I work five hours a day, and there is enough of everything. I am blissfully happy."

I could not get that story out of my head for several days. It was then that I realised that I could read all the theory of organization, communication, and marketing, and pass all that theoretical knowledge onto others. **However, success is not hidden in books, but in the heart of the individual. There is only one formula for success: Work with your heart!**

We should never push anything in life; and most importantly, the goal should never be money. Everything that we do should be to our joy, from life with the person we live with, the work we do, to the people who surround us. Nowhere should we feel overwhelmed or like we are doing something for the sake of others.

In changing ourselves, we sometimes encounter resistance from our surrounding environment. It could be the wife, husband, parents, or friends. What to do in that case? Many people say that they would rather keep their marriage than replace their current job, which does not fulfil them with one they would adore. They would rather suffer at work, as long as they do not lose their wives. However, such a decision destroys a person even more in the long run and takes away their life energy. Yes, they will save the marriage, but inside, they will suffer more and more, become increasingly tired of life, and lose in their eye. And maybe, only maybe, it will ultimately (and ironically) become the exact reason their spouse leaves them.

That is why it is crucial, and always most important, to find our happiness within ourselves. Let us find what makes us happy and fulfils us. How the surroundings react to that is not our responsibility nor concern. Let us do everything in our power to keep everything we love. But if it does not work, let it go. Your own happiness should always — ALWAYS — come first.

No matter how much, and in what way our surroundings change, in the long run, this approach is always the path to happiness, both inside and outside the individual.

And that is really the only way out of our current *crisis*. Everyone should do what they really love doing and should surround themselves with those they really love. Do your work with your heart, because only you can give your best and always set higher goals that will help you to develop continuously and grow both in your career as well as your personality.

So, listen to the desires of your heart, listen to yourself and your inner drives! Everything else will sooner or later adapt to the happiness you radiate. Trust that everything will fall into place.

Wherever I go,
wherever I am,
the same person
is always with
me: ME.

WHY? DON'T ASK YOURSELF THAT!

You have probably already heard the classic piece of advice on personal growth and finding the path to happiness: "Always ask yourself—WHY you are doing something, WHY you are what you are, WHY ..."

We ask ourselves WHY only when we do not know ourselves well enough.

We ask ourselves WHY when we are uncertain about something. However, if we know ourselves well, if we do not doubt ourselves, then we know exactly what we need to do. I am talking about the inner voice, the intuition, the potential about who we really are, and where only we know ourselves well enough to do things without having second thoughts. Where empty space, doubt and mistrust arise, there we will always first ask ourselves, "WHY?"

The question WHY can otherwise be prevention, like a fuse in electricity, that protects us from doing something *foolish* and jumping heedlessly into some business, project or even marriage.

This brings forward the question of how much we really know ourselves, and how much we trust ourselves.

Of course, it is still better to ask WHY than make a fatal mistake.

The question WHY takes up a lot of our time since it opens up countless doubts, making us to start doing various analyses, yet we are ultimately still unsure, and keep wondering why, why, why ...

For that reason, the right path would be to start raising us in the spirit of self-cognition, perception of own needs, and above all, communication about what we want, what we like ... But how?

There is nothing wrong with the question WHY? Still, it is only the third level thinking and perception of the surrounding environment.

If you first ask yourself, “WHO AM I, WHAT DO I FEEL?” you will never doubt yourself again, and you will also never again ask yourself “WHY?”

You will simply know! You will trust yourself!

One morning,
when you wake up,
you stop looking,
because everything
is here.

BIGGEST STRANGERS TO OURSELVES

We are a complete stranger to ourselves. And we do everything to escape from ourselves.

Knowing ourselves is the basis of everything we do. Everything we do in life is the basis of our decision-making, where we make decisions based on what we feel. This is where the problem arises since most people do not know how to distinguish their own feelings from the feelings of others in them. Moreover, many people have several feelings that they do not know how to differentiate, thus ending up not knowing which feeling is real. Few people know exactly what they feel, what they want, and who they are. Everything stems from knowing yourself.

If we know ourselves well and know what we want to do, we will also know what kind of a partner we want next to us and what kind of people we want to socialize. At first glance, life becomes simpler. But in fact, it means that we have found the inner peace we all long.

High self-awareness is actually the process of creating inner peace.

It is difficult to *fix* yourself, therefore, it is recommended that we have someone to show us the mirror from time to time or guide us through the process. In doing so, we must be careful not to become dependent on that person, but rather treat as temporary support. **The basic foundation is one's own desire for change**.

If we pay attention to external signs and know how to interpret them, they can be an excellent guide to that change - helping us shape ourselves and make progress, so we should never understand them as a personal attack or something negative, because such resistance could cost us several years of life.

The core message of book is self-awareness. Dealing with other people wastes our precious and limited time we have in this world. And time represents the only real asset (capital) which we are given at the beginning of life. The more we know ourselves, the easier for us to manage our time and life.

Life is, in fact, a
love story.
The continuation
and end always
depend on the
author of the
story.

THE PERSONAL TRANSFORMATION METHOD

The method of personal transformation is intended for creating the inner peace we all strive to achieve. Some travel the world, others find refuge in different temples, stimulants, and rituals. In reality, we all have everything at hand; it is just that we do not realise it because we are in too much of a hurry to find a solution.

We are looking for some key, the holy grail, the moment in which we will experience enlightenment. And from then on, nothing will be difficult for us anymore.

I have travelled almost the whole world and gone through all kinds of efforts in trying to experience revelation, and finally, I did find it. However, it happened only after I rested and tidied up everything. I had started over the years but never finished, such as studies, projects, books, and business relations that developed into legal disputes.

Finding inner peace is about balance — the balance between the body, intellect, emotions, and soul.

You will notice that it is sometimes necessary to make a big turn to get to the essence. **Shortcuts are the greatest distraction of inner**

peace. The quicker we want to achieve inner peace, the further we move away from it.

Before anything, we should first calm down, which means that we should put aside all activities and do absolutely nothing. Even those who think they are doing nothing, are in fact doing a lot when watching television, listening to the radio news report, or reading bad news -- all are distractions.

The model is based on getting to know oneself! However, we do not get to know ourselves by looking at ourselves in the mirror, but rather through our actions. Here I would like to mention a thought of Martin Kojc, "The material world is a reflection of our thoughts!" Everything that happens around us is in fact a reflection of our inner selves.

That is why we need to take a slightly different look at our surroundings and perceive them as though they are important messages – a warning that we need to start doing things in another way because we are heading down the wrong road and are probably approaching a wall. For this reason, in the continuation, a few checklists are laid down to remind us of the things that are happening around us.

CLEANING AND TIDYING UP

The first step is intended to clean or tidy up. And I do not mean only the usual tidying of drawers, cabinets, but of everything material that we have not used for more than two years and of anything that seems useless to us or invokes any kind of negative emotions in us. When I mention cleaning, I also consider littered thoughts: unnecessary information, unnecessary loads, and unnecessary habits.

Physical tidying up also means changing certain habits. Among them are morning rituals, daily routes we use to get to work, or to the cafes we frequent. If possible, we should rearrange our furniture, and change the colours of our walls, style of dressing, and our food.

Changes should be introduced gradually. With drastic overnight changes, the result is the opposite of what we would like.

When we get rid of the unnecessary littering, we get a clear view of everything we have not seen so far.

CLEAN UP YOUR PSYCHOLOGICAL LITTER

Of course, changes are not necessary if you consider that you feel great and that everything is fine. However, if something is not running smoothly in any area of your life, it means that you are out of balance. In that case, it is necessary to first find the cause of your imbalance. And the cause can only be found by tidying everything up and removing anything that obscures our view.

Our current way of life has actually been governed by someone else. If our life was governed using our own free will, we would not be looking for a solution.

And that is exactly what we are aiming at — taking matters into our own hands and becoming masters of our own destiny. This way, every time we make a decision, we feel calm and without external pressure.

As already written at the beginning of the book, a large part of our life is linked to our birth and early upbringing. We are not born with instructions for life, instead we could say that at birth we get a camera that records how our surroundings live. It records the reactions of those close to us, their reactions in certain moments, but above all, whether people in the surroundings live in accordance with their feelings or not. If we are raised in a *free* environment, in which people express their feelings, then we get the permission to develop our potentials. If that is not the case, the potentials get banned from developing. Dust begins to collect on our potential. That is what we refer to as *psychological litter*. Such waste is a collection of films recorded by that camera, and we begin to live by this scenario, which is filled with prohibitions and the reflections of the authorities who raised us.

This life scenario needs constant validation that it is living properly. This is why it will choose certain friends, positions, lifestyle, wall colours, hair colour, and ways to work. In short, almost everything we do, we do because of the scenario written for us by someone else. This scenario could also be named the Trojan horse in our subconscious. It can, therefore, be said that we live someone else's life, not our own.

If we wish to erase this scenario and start living what we feel deep inside, we must gradually begin to change the scenario. But how? By starting to slowly take away its "validations," that is, its psychological food. What makes the process of changing habits so hard is that we have to starve the life scenario out. But keep in mind, it will fight for survival until the very end. And that is usually the main reason why so many give up, as the path proves to be too strenuous for them leaving them to surrender to the current created for them by others.

In other words, cleansing is intended to remove the psychological food from someone else's scenario by which we live.

On the following pages, I demonstrate psychology exercises and guidelines that allow us to find the path to ourselves.

DISCOVERING YOURSELF

When we begin to gradually change the physical world around us, it is time to start getting to know ourselves. What is then our own scenario? What drives it?

The simplest method to find the answers to the two questions above is to look at the persons who are emotionally close to us as at ourselves. These can be the persons we either currently live with or who we grew up with, they can also be friends or even complete strangers. What matters is that it is the persons who when we think of them evoke a certain emotion in us—happiness, joy, anger, sadness, or love.

Find five such individuals. Write their names on a piece of paper. For each of them, write their positive and negative qualities. And then put that paper away for five days.

Five days later, read the qualities as if they were all your own. Circle the ones you believe do not apply to you. Then put the paper away again for three days.

In three days, read the circled qualities again. Read them as if they were your own. Circle again the ones you are absolutely convinced are not yours.

The qualities circled twice represent your reflection of the characteristics that are hidden in your scenario.

Already by reading the double circled qualities, we activate the process of change, since we start thinking about those qualities hard, causing their power to decrease every day.

In this context, it is important that we start to get to know ourselves in other areas as well.

TAKE CARE OF THE PHYSICAL BODY

After we have cleaned up our environment, we have to start dealing with the physical body. The body is like a machine that needs regular maintenance. Food is the body's fuel; nevertheless, the latter should be of the highest quality for the body to function properly.

There is no universal answer to the question of which sport is the right one and which food is healthy, as each person is a different story. Therefore, each person should consult an expert based on beforehand analyses. Keep in mind that you should not start too fast; instead, start researching, try different sports, and the right one for you will be the one which makes you feel confident and gives you joy. You do not need to look at others nor feel guilty because someone runs every morning, while you dance tango only twice a week. What matters is to stay in motion.

It is similar with food. It is important for the body to get the necessary amounts of ingredients it needs during the day, but the most important thing is that you enjoy your food. And there are experts for that too. Fast food is certainly not very healthy, because we should be aware that we take food directly into the body and in the same way in which it was prepared. We transfer that energy directly into our body. So, pay attention to how your food is prepared and who prepares it.

Before you start making changes in the physiological field, I always recommend that you consult a physician – and I mean a conventional medicine doctor – for an examination of the physical body that includes:

- blood tests for hormone balance,

- spinal imaging of primarily the atlas — the first cervical vertebra of the spine,
- cardiac imaging, as modern diseases are hidden in the heart,
- entire cardiovascular system imaging, and
- brain imaging.

Such thorough examination shows the physical boundaries of an individual, and whether certain psychological habits really cannot be changed due to psychological patterns in the individual's life scenario, or the problem lies solely in the disturbed balance or some hidden defect. This way, we also find out where the limitations of our own body are and get a recommendation on which physical activity we can engage in, as well as which food to consume to ensure additional energy to our body.

If you want to be happy,
do not look for the best,
because
you will never come to
the end.
Get the best out of
what you have.

WORK ON YOURSELF

Working on yourself is not only doing sports, reading books, and visiting spiritual workshops, but rather a holistic approach and striving for balance.

STEP ONE: WORK ON THE BODY (FOOD, MOVEMENT)

The brain represents the central organ behind all activities, which needs a sufficient amount of oxygen and enough fresh blood. The higher the brain load, the higher the consumption. And if the body is not maintained enough, it cannot provide the brain with the necessary amounts of quality oxygen and blood. In this case, the brain sends information to the body to slow down, and suddenly we become tired and lazy. This is because the brain will make sure that there is always enough of what it needs, even to the detriment of other organs and bodily functions.

As personal transformation is an emotionally strenuous process, it is important that the physical body is strong enough to withstand the strain.

Regular and quality physical activity as well as quality nutrition are extremely important for enduring with ease all the necessary activities.

And work on the body is only a quarter of everything that needs to be done.

STEP TWO: INTELLECT

The second quarter is our intellect, or, in other words, our brain again. Since we spend most of the day dealing with a particular problem or the same types of problems, the brain becomes "imbalanced" and needs to be counterbalanced. In the second part of the day, it makes sense to introduce some mental exercise, perhaps playing a video game, reading a book, studying something from a completely different area, doing crossword puzzles or mind games ... anything but watching television. From time to time, it is welcome if we watch some creative content or follow the news important for everyday life, while I advise against anything else.

And so, we have come halfway through the steps. We are slowly establishing balance at all levels.

STEP THREE: EMOTIONS

Our emotions come third. And I do not mean love, romance, or art – these are actually entertainment. What I mean is that we need to start researching where we are entertained. Above all, we need to observe in what exactly we are entertained in everyday activities, or better, in what we find naturalness and playfulness. In short – where we find enjoyment.

STEP FOUR: SOUL

In conclusion, we have our soul. It is actually peacefulness, a retreat in which we focus on ourselves. For some, it is prayer, for others meditation, for someone else beer after work or a walk in nature. In short, it is about the time that we dedicate to ourselves only and in which we can focus on our thoughts.

ACCOMPLISHING INNER PEACE

If we start working on these four components parallel to each other, we will take a step forward towards accomplishing inner peace. If, on the other hand, we deal with one or two only, we will not make much progress because of the other two components. That will lead us to spin even further in circles, and it will become harder and harder for us. To illustrate with an example: if we only play sports, we will eventually run a marathon or an even longer distance, in other words, we will constantly seek for more and more effort, but never establish inner peace.

Within days, all activities must be evenly fulfilled with approximately equal intensity.

"Where do we find the time for all that?" you might say. We have time. However, in order to avoid panic and confusion, it is important that you start introducing changes and work on yourself gradually, and within the scope of what you are already doing. But above all, keep in mind that by doing it slowly and patiently, you will reach the goal much sooner than by looking for shortcuts.

When you establish balance and find satisfaction in every area, it does not yet mean that the process is over. It is actually only then that the process truly begins.

When within the context of all these components we start discovering what we like, we suddenly start having fun and become more and more focused on ourselves. Unexpectedly, we are no longer interested in the outside world, but instead so much more on our inner world. In a way, we put up a fence against all the negative influences we have had until that point, because we simply do not see them anymore. That is how we spontaneously stop dealing with negative things. Instead, we start dealing with our energy only.

Now we have stepped on the path to inner peace. That peace must be continuously maintained. How? By enjoying everyday activities. And eventually, you will never do anything you do not enjoy again.

In the end,
we all come
to the same.
Only
feelings that
you have chosen
yourself in life
matter.

WITH SIMPLE EXERCISES TO KEY ANSWERS

To make the journey to key answers easier, I recommend starting with the following exercise. On your mobile phone, set three alarms at different times in the same day. When the alarm rings, ask yourself: "WHO AM I?" and "WHAT DO I FEEL?" Do not look for answers just ask yourself. Keep repeating this throughout the process until, in seeking an activity, you feel your first passion. The answers to the two questions will begin to appear on their own, entirely spontaneously and when you least expect them (every day over three weeks at least). That is why you should not bother to look for them at all. Let it happen naturally and on its own.

With this exercise, you wake up the forgotten emotions that were suppressed in your early childhood.

At the same time, add the following exercise: **appointments with yourself**. Every morning ask yourself how you want to feel at the end of the day. If that is not the feeling you have at the end of the day, have an appointment with yourself. In the appointment, analyse the whole day, and you will see which activities prevented you from feeling that. This means that those activities take away your energy.

Start changing or removing them.

With the last exercise, you are focused on one day at a time. Become aware of the start and end of the day. That is how you actively start and consciously end the day. You start living one day at a time.

By accomplishing balance this way, a number of unnecessary things in life fall away, including those we thought were absolutely necessary for success. We quickly realise that they are in fact an obstacle to happiness.

SEVEN NATURAL PHASES OF THE PATH TO CHANGE

By observing natural phenomena in the laboratory (first as a secondary school student of metallurgy and then a university student of physics), I noticed that seven phases always take place —when an element changes its structure or energy gets a higher frequency, taking a step back is no longer possible. In other words, we can no longer restore the original structure of the material nor give the energy back lower frequency. In modern physics we call this a quantum leap.

When I finished reality therapy studies and was in the middle of transactional analysis studies, I discovered in even more detail how the human conscious and subconscious mind (human psychology) works. It quickly became clear to me that if you want to change a habit, you have to make a firm decision and stick to it no matter what. But, how to achieve that? Although I had been surrounded by psychology for several years, I was still thinking like a technician. A technician always looks for ultimate solutions; and I was certain there had to be some procedures and precise parameters. But I could not find them anywhere. Yes, taught us a clearly defined system of how to conduct a conversation as a psychotherapist, however, it was based on developing own experience. Psychotherapy is building a relationship and healing through that relationship. Yet, I was thinking: a psychotherapist would need a certain map so as not to get lost.

Thus, my psychotherapeutic brain itself began to look for a technical solution on how a person makes a decision and by doing so makes a radical change.

Since I already had some experience with almost clients, I browsed through my notes to study the changes in their behaviour. I also observed new clients, what method I was guiding them by, what was happening to them, and how much time they needed for a change. I realised that certain things could be very clearly—technically—defined.

In fact, in the background of a conversation between the client and the psychotherapist, there is advanced mathematics without us being aware of it.

This is how I found the seven steps of transformation in nature and applied them to psychotherapy. I began to realise that clients also behaved like matter/element or energy in a particular phase. Their steps and behaviour were very similar. When I brought the clients to the end of the process of change and transformation, they transitioned into a new state. My clients became different as if the previous state had never existed. In fact, they could not believe that they actually had a problem, nor could they ever again return to their previous state.

In internal development, the quantum leap is the moment we notice in ourselves a deep and final shift in emotions and behaviour and then we realise that something has changed forever.

An external observer could just as well say that these clients simply made a decision. However, it is exactly decision making that is crucial to a person's life. We make 35,000 decisions every day. That means we go through the mentioned seven steps 35,000 times a day without even being aware of it.

Occasionally, we skip one of the seven phases and consequently get stuck. We then get the feeling that we are spinning in circles, which can take years. This is where a psychotherapist can help us get out of that vicious circle.

Based on all the acquired observations and good knowledge of natural phenomena, I developed a method that I named the **Sirius Personal Transformation.**

I will not describe the individual phases more specifically as they are already described in great detail of the book titled, *Me.* If you prefer, you can learn about and experience them also in a 75-hour training. For more information, please visit www.dynamicleadership.management/.

THE FIRST THREE PHASES ARE INTENDED FOR ANALYSIS.

To be able to analyse something, we must first tidy things up, as seen in one of the stories in this book. However, that is only the first phase. Only after we tidy up the things can we see where we are and what it is that we actually need.

Then, in the second phase, we remove everything that is not ours, what we consider no longer belonging to us. In life, we experience it as a salvation, a relief, when we get the feeling of having experienced enlightenment. But in fact, we only made room for fresh energy. If we do not quickly take a few steps forward at that stage, our burden will become greater than the one we have borne until then.

This is why, in the third phase, we need to think about what brought us to this point and what we want, how to now fill that free space, but it could also be that free space itself is enough for us on its own. It is important that we arrange all remaining things so that we have the feeling of being in balance.

However, the feeling of excitement begins to disappear and is replaced by the feeling of anxiety. We start thinking about how much time, energy, and money that we have lost. We say things like *what was I thinking*, or *I was so blind* and similar cries of remorse.

That is why we must never stop in the third phase, in which we also finalise the analysis.

IN THE FOURTH PHASE, WE SET A NEW GOAL.

Where do we want to go next, based on the new feelings and new knowledge about ourselves? Anxiety is still present in this phase, and there is also guilt because we feel we are betraying someone by moving on. That is why intensive physical activity is necessary for the body and brain to get enough oxygen for us to cope with the psychological efforts more easily. Although we are slowly setting ourselves a new path, the energy of old habits is still very present and keeps pulling us back. This is why we must have good stamina, so we do not succumb to all those voices persuading us to quit.

IN THE FIFTH PHASE, WE INTENSIVELY DEAL WITH BREAKING OLD HABITS.

This is where we usually change the people, we socialize with and almost everything that hinders us in expressing our own will. It of course depends on the degree of transformation we are in and the area in which we perform the transformation. While we might be making a minor change, such as quitting smoking, by doing so, we are actually addressing 100 other subconscious setbacks. The fifth phase is most intense, but in it we already start feeling relief, despite having the feeling that there is a storm around us.

IN THE SIXTH PHASE, WE SET A NEW PATH.

In this phase, we say that *there is sunshine after the rain* since we start laying down the path towards the desired feelings. At this point, the calls from the past can barely be heard - are already treading the new path.

THE SEVENTH PHASE – THE NEW PATH.

In the last phase, the new path has almost entirely become a part of our life, and we lose the feeling that we have changed something, even though the surroundings tell us that we are different. We often do not notice these changes ourselves because we are in the centre of the happening, while the people around us see a significant change. We feel the changes much earlier, but when we calm down completely in the final phase, we do not know anymore what it was even about, although it happened yesterday.

The same process of transformation is available also for companies — the Sirius Business Transformation — however, under the condition that the person carrying out the transformation has previously undergone the process of personal transformation. For more information, visit www.dynamicleadership.management.

You cannot
change nature.
You can only
understand it.

In the end, we
realise that true success lies in
one's own satisfaction.
Inner peace
through
our own activities.
Success is thus not
what others value
in us.
The real success
is to be happy.

HAPPY WE!

ABOUT DYNAMILOGY

Dynamilogy is the active study of "living" processes and phenomena related to human and nature. It is a new branch of science that I formed based on physics, psychology, and economics.

It is decoding of nature's secrets of a sort. Only if we look at nature, we see that everything is simple, that everything works on its own. And we often say that it would be great if it was like that also in our lives.

Let us examine a diamond as an example. A diamond is made of carbon. But graphite is also made of carbon. The difference between the two is only in the atomic structure. And if we transfer this fact to our economy, how much graphite would we have to sell to get a value that is equal to the value of one sold diamond?

The whole secret is therefore in the right order. The code of nature is the right order. If we compare a business process or a process in personal life with natural processes, we quickly figure out what we are doing wrong. This way we will also quickly come up with a formula for success. All we need to do is to put the process in our personal or business life in the right order.

And in the end, you will realize that happiness is just a decision!

The aim of dynamilogy is to put a person before work and to reverse the course of the current chaos in the world.

The following models are derived from dynamilogy:

1. The Dynamic Leadership Model, a business methodology that puts people first.
2. The Dynamic Leadership Model for Administrative Systems on a Local Level, which puts the potential of the environment and people first.
3. The Dynamic Communication Model, which creates a refined flow of information.
4. Sirius Personal Transformation, a psychological method of self-discovery.
5. Sirius Business Transformation, a business methodology of process reform.
6. Project Office, a form of enterprise organisation with projects and project management as basic elements, representing a completely natural process.
7. Dynamic Circle, organisation of one's own life in order to accomplish inner peace.
8. Dynamic Leader, a New Age business profession.
9. Dynamic Manager, a New Age business management profession.
10. Dynamic Engineer, a New Age profession for personality-based process planning.

www.Dynamilogy.ch

ABOUT THE AUTHOR

Prof. Dr. Milan Krajnc is nominated for the Nobel Prize in Economics 2021. He founded the new scientific science *Dynamilogy*, which unlocked the secrets of nature and from this created a new business model (*Dynamic Leadership Model*) that stimulates the natural needs of people. However, with the development of primary human needs and feelings, the world economy begins to change; because the economy is based on consumption needs. With the *Dynamic Leadership Model* he has structured all the processes very precisely, combining the laws of physics, psychology and implementing them in the economics of needs.

He is a full professor of Public Management at the European Center for Peace and Development, the University of Peace established by the United Nations in Professor of Economic Sciences and representative of Al-Khalifa Business School in the Principality of Monaco.

For the last 15 years he has been running a private practice in the field of psychotherapy. He has been solving crisis situations in companies and family businesses for 20 years. He has written more than 300 books in the field of leadership and relationships and more than 200 professional and scientific articles; the latest work entitled

"Dynamic Leadership Model" has already been translated into 11 foreign languages and is still being translated into several languages.

Sincerely about me: "I will not alter my self-image in order to appear successful in the eyes of others.

Before I started "selling the theory", I created a lot as an entrepreneur and later also lost a lot, only to then create even more.

Before I started "developing the theory", I read numerous books, spent hours on end in the laboratory, and above all, experienced and survived many life's blows.

Before I started teaching the theory to students, I tested it countless times in practice.

I would also like YOU to be HAPPY, so that peace may rule the world."

e-mail: dr@MilanKrajnc.ch

LIBRARYofMK

Library of Milan Krajnc

library.mk

milankrajnc

Library of Milan Krajnc (LibraryMK)

www.milankrajnc.com